READING POWER

American Tycoons

J. Pierpont Morgan

and Wall Street

Lewis K. Parker

The Rosen Publishing Group's
PowerKids Press™
New York

Published in 2003 by The Rosen Publishing Group, Inc.
29 East 21st Street, New York, NY 10010

First Edition

Book Design: Daniel Hosek

Photo Credits: Cover © National Portrait Gallery, Smithsonian Institution/Art Resource, NY; pp. 4, 5, 7, 8, 9, 10, 12, 13, 16, 21 courtesy of the Archives, The Pierpont Morgan Library, New York/Art Resource, NY; pp. 11, 14–15, 17 © North Wind Picture Archives; p. 18 Library of Congress, Prints and Photographs Division; p. 19 © Bettmann/Corbis; p. 20 © Corbis

Library of Congress Cataloging-in-Publication Data

Parker, Lewis K.
J. Pierpont Morgan and Wall Street / Lewis K. Parker.
    p. cm. — (American tycoons)
Summary: A short biography of investor and stockbrocker, J. Pierpont Morgan.
Includes bibliographical references (p.) and index.
ISBN 0-8239-6449-3 (library bdg.)
1. Morgan, J. Pierpont (John Pierpont), 1837-1913—Juvenile literature. 2. Bankers—United States—Biography—Juvenile literature. 3. Capitalists and financiers—United States—Biography—Juvenile literature. [1. Morgan, J. Pierpont (John Pierpont), 1837-1913. 2. Bankers. 3. Capitalists and financiers.] I. Title.
HG2463.M6 P37 2003
332.1'092—dc21

2002000114

Contents

The Early Years

J. Pierpont Morgan was one of America's most successful tycoons. He ran many important companies. One of Morgan's companies, the United States Steel Corporation, was the first company in the world to be worth $1 billion.

John Pierpont Morgan was born on April 17, 1837, in Hartford, Connecticut. His father, Junius Morgan, was a successful banker.

Junius Morgan trained J. Pierpont Morgan to take over his banking business.

Junius Morgan

4

J. Pierpont Morgan is shown (center) with two of his sisters—Sarah (left) and Mary (right).

Check It Out

J. Pierpont Morgan's uncle, James Pierpont, wrote the song "One Horse Open Sleigh," which later came to be known as "Jingle Bells."

J. Pierpont Morgan went to college in Germany. Then he worked as a clerk in his father's banking office in London, England.

In 1857, Morgan went to New York City. There, he worked for the U.S. office of his father's banking business.

When Morgan began his work as a clerk, there were no copy machines or typewriters. Morgan had to copy all business papers by hand.

Family Ties

In 1860, Morgan married Amelia Sturges. She died four months after they got married. In 1865, he married Frances Tracy. The Morgans had four children: J.P. Morgan, Jr., Louisa, Juliet, and Anne.

J. Pierpont Morgan was a successful banker and businessman throughout his career.

Frances Morgan was known to her family and friends as "Fanny."

Big Business

In 1885, Morgan started working with railroad companies. He decided how these companies would be run and who would run them. Soon, Morgan controlled many railroads. He became very powerful.

J. Pierpont Morgan was a large man, with cold eyes and a fearsome frown. He would not work with men he disliked.

Morgan gave money to Thomas Edison to help with Edison's inventions. Morgan brought Edison General Electric Company together with another electric company to make General Electric. He gained control over this company, too.

Thomas Edison's inventions and discoveries changed the lives of people around the world. Edison invented the light bulb and the movie camera.

In 1890, J. Pierpont Morgan's father, Junius Morgan, died. Morgan took over his father's banking business. In 1895, J. Pierpont Morgan started a new company by joining his father's business with Drexel, Morgan and Company. It was called J.P. Morgan & Company. The company quickly became one of the most powerful banking companies in the world.

Anthony J. Drexel, Sr. was J. Pierpont Morgan's business partner.

J. Pierpont Morgan had his offices in the Drexel Building in New York City.

In 1895, the U.S. government was about to run out of gold. J. Pierpont Morgan and other businessmen traded $65 million in gold for U.S. government bonds. Morgan then sold the bonds for more money. People called him a robber baron because he made so much money from the deal.

President Grover Cleveland (shown in picture) asked Morgan and other businessmen to help the government when it needed money.

"A man always has two reasons for doing anything—a good reason and the real reason."

—J. Pierpont Morgan

The Big Deal

In 1901, Morgan paid $480 million for Andrew Carnegie's steel company. This was more money than the U.S. government spent in a year! He joined Carnegie's steel company with ten others to form the U.S. Steel Corporation. It was the largest corporation in the world.

This paper shows that J. Pierpont Morgan owned a part of the U.S. Steel Corporation.

After selling his steel company to J. Pierpont Morgan, Andrew Carnegie became the richest man in the world.

J.Pierpont Morgan gained control and power in these companies:

- New York Central Railroad
- Pennsylvania Railroad
- Southern Railroad
- Erie Railroad
- Northern Pacific Railroad
- General Electric
- U.S. Steel
- AT&T
- International Harvester

Morgan's Gifts to the World

Morgan died on March 31, 1913, in Rome, Italy. During his lifetime, Morgan gave money to help build churches, hospitals, and art museums. He also spent millions of dollars collecting art and books. After he died, many of Morgan's books and much of his art collection were given to libraries and museums.

J. Pierpont Morgan's personal library, which was next to his home in New York City, is now a public library.

Morgan gave money to build the Cathedral of St. John the Divine in New York City.

Check It Out

When he was fourteen years old, Morgan sent a card to President Millard Fillmore. Morgan asked the president to sign the card and return it to him. The president did it. This was one of the first things that Morgan ever collected.

J. Pierpont Morgan was worth about $119 million when he died. That would be about $25 billion today. He was very powerful in the American banking and business communities. He was the greatest banker of his time.

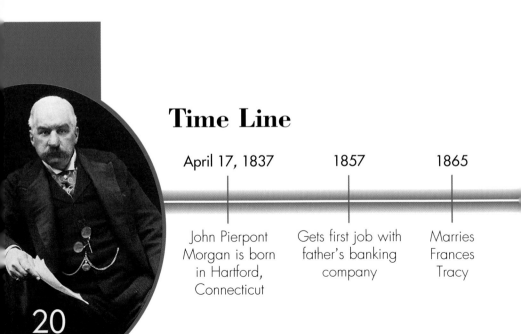

Time Line

April 17, 1837	1857	1865
John Pierpont Morgan is born in Hartford, Connecticut	Gets first job with father's banking company	Marries Frances Tracy

In his spare time, J. Pierpont Morgan liked to sail his boats.

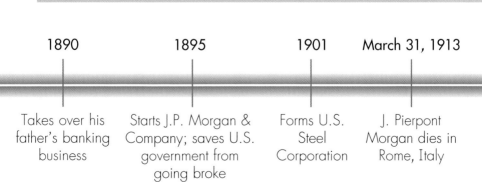

1890	1895	1901	March 31, 1913
Takes over his father's banking business	Starts J.P. Morgan & Company; saves U.S. government from going broke	Forms U.S. Steel Corporation	J. Pierpont Morgan dies in Rome, Italy

Glossary

bonds (**bahndz**) things a government or business sells in order to raise money

clerk (**klerk**) someone who does office work, especially by keeping records

college (**kahl**-ihj) a school where people can study after high school

corporation (kor-puh-**ray**-shuhn) a large company that makes, buys, or sells things

inventions (ihn-**vehn**-shuhnz) new things that someone thinks of or makes

museums (myoo-**zee**-uhmz) places where objects are shown or studied

robber baron (**rahb**-uhr **bar**-uhn) a powerful person who has made a lot of money by treating others poorly

tycoons (ty-**koonz**) businesspeople with a lot of wealth and power

Resources

Books

An Age of Extremes, 1870–1917
by Joy Hakim
Oxford University Press (1999)

Famous Financiers and Innovators
by Norman L. Macht
Chelsea House Publishers (2001)

Web Sites

Due to the changing nature of Internet links, PowerKids Press has developed an on-line list of Web sites related to the subjects of this book. This site is updated regularly. Please use this link to access the list:

http://www.powerkidslinks.com/aty/jpm/

Index

Word Count: 497
Note to Librarians, Teachers, and Parents

If reading is a challenge, Reading Power is a solution! Reading Power is perfect for readers who want high-interest subject matter at an accessible reading level. These fact-filled, photo-illustrated books are designed for readers who want straightforward vocabulary, engaging topics, and a manageable reading experience. With clear picture/text correspondence, leveled Reading Power books put the reader in charge. Now readers have the power to get the information they want and the skills they need in a user-friendly format.